FOCUS ON CURRENT EVENTS

RACISM

by Anitra Budd

T0400827

WE ARE EQUAL

NO JUSTICE

FOCUS READERS.

VOYAGER

www.focusreaders.com

Copyright © 2024 by Focus Readers®, Lake Elmo, MN 55042. All rights reserved. No part of this book may be reproduced or utilized in any form or by any means without written permission from the publisher.

Focus Readers is distributed by North Star Editions:
sales@northstareditions.com | 888-417-0195

Produced for Focus Readers by Red Line Editorial.

Content Consultant: James M. Thomas, PhD, Associate Professor of Sociology, The University of Mississippi

Photographs ©: iStockphoto, cover, 1, 7, 10–11, 27, 28–29, 39, 40–41, 44; Dita Alangkara/AP Images, 4–5; Ramon Espinosa/AP Images, 9; Schomburg Center for Research in Black Culture/Photographs and Prints Division/The New York Public Library, 13; Jack Harris/AP Images, 15; Alexandra Wimley/Pittsburgh Post-Gazette/AP Images, 17; Shutterstock Images, 18–19, 34–35; Richard Drew/AP Images, 21; Matilde Campodonico/AP Images, 23; Russell Lee/Farm Security Administration/Office of War Information Photograph Collection/Library of Congress, 24–25; Red Line Editorial, 30, 36; Rogelio V. Solis/AP Images, 33; Jeff Wheeler/The Star Tribune/AP Images, 43

Library of Congress Cataloging-in-Publication Data
Names: Budd, Anitra, author.
Title: Racism / by Anitra Budd.
Description: Lake Elmo, MN : Focus Readers, [2024] | Series: Focus on
   current events | Includes index. | Audience: Grades 4-6
Identifiers: LCCN 2023003201 (print) | LCCN 2023003202 (ebook) | ISBN
   9781637396445 (hardcover) | ISBN 9781637397015 (paperback) | ISBN
   9781637398081 (pdf) | ISBN 9781637397589 (ebook)
Subjects: LCSH: Racism--History--Juvenile literature.
Classification: LCC HT1521 .B733 2024 (print) | LCC HT1521 (ebook) | DDC
   305.8--dc23/eng/20230202
LC record available at https://lccn.loc.gov/2023003201
LC ebook record available at https://lccn.loc.gov/2023003202

Printed in the United States of America
Mankato, MN
082023

ABOUT THE AUTHOR

Anitra Budd is a writer, editor, and educator. She has written books and articles for young people and adults. She enjoys reading, sewing, and learning new languages.

TABLE OF CONTENTS

CHAPTER 1
What Is Racism? 5

CHAPTER 2
Racism Through History 11

CASE STUDY
Anti-Asian Violence 16

CHAPTER 3
Criminal Justice 19

CHAPTER 4
Housing and Wealth 25

CHAPTER 5
Health and Medicine 29

CHAPTER 6
Education 35

CASE STUDY
The CROWN Act 38

CHAPTER 7
Fighting Racism 41

Focus on Racism • 46
Glossary • 47
To Learn More • 48
Index • 48

CHAPTER 1

WHAT IS RACISM?

Serena Williams is known around the world as a tennis champion. But in September 2017, she was simply a Black woman having a baby, and she was scared.

Six years earlier, Williams had suffered from blood clots in her lungs. This condition can be deadly if untreated. After Williams gave birth, she felt worried. She thought the blood clots might have returned. She asked the hospital staff to

In early 2017, Serena Williams won her 23rd major championship. She was pregnant at the time.

run tests. But no one listened to her. One nurse even told her she sounded crazy.

Williams kept asking for help. Finally, a doctor discovered that Williams was right. A scan showed a new blood clot in her lungs. Fortunately, Williams got better after surgery. She was able to go home with her daughter a few days later. But she didn't forget how the doctors and nurses had treated her.

Later, Williams wrote an essay about what happened. She noted the statistics on childbirth. Black women were three times more likely to die than white women. Williams said the statistics could change. But for that to happen, health-care providers would need to listen to Black women.

What Williams experienced that day was racism. To learn about racism, it's important to first understand race. Race is a system that puts

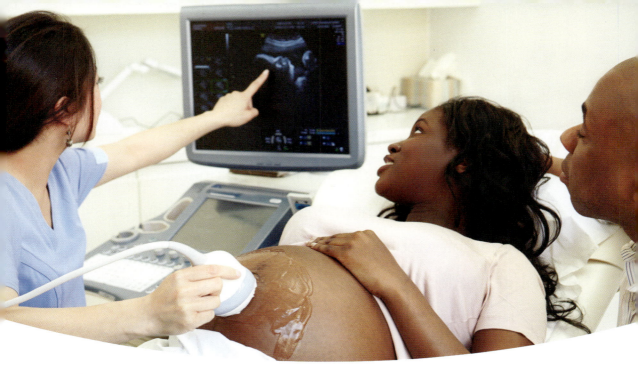

⚠ Williams wrote about how being listened to by health-care workers during pregnancy can be a matter of life or death.

humans into different groups based on their physical differences. It is often based on skin color. Race can also involve hair texture, facial features, and more. Race gives meaning to these different groups. It affects people across society.

However, race is not based on science or nature. Race is a human invention. It is only significant because of racism.

Racism is when people give others unfair privileges or penalties based on race. Some people might imagine only interpersonal racism. This is racism that happens between individuals. An example would be a teacher allowing only white students to retake a test for a higher grade.

However, there are many different kinds of racism. Institutional racism is a second main kind. That's when racism is woven into rules and practices of organizations. This can happen at the level of one company. Suppose a business refused to hire people with traditionally Chinese names. That rule would be institutional racism.

Institutional racism is also part of larger things such as the law. Racism is woven into many parts of the law. For example, Puerto Rico is a US territory, not a state. Nearly all people in Puerto Rico are Latino. People born in Puerto Rico

▲ Because Puerto Rico is a territory, it tends to receive less disaster aid than states, and the aid is often delayed.

are US citizens. But they cannot vote in federal elections. They receive far less in government benefits. This is also institutional racism.

Systemic racism is a third type. It involves all parts of a society. They include government, the economy, laws, schools, and more. All these parts work together to enforce racism. These systems often reflect the society's racist cultural beliefs. Systemic racism is the most widespread form of racism. It is also the hardest to eliminate.

CHAPTER 2

RACISM THROUGH HISTORY

Race as we know it today didn't always exist. People invented it centuries ago. They did so to create and maintain power and wealth.

In the 1600s, European scientists were building new systems to categorize plants and animals. Over time, they began applying categories to human beings. Around the same time, Europeans were traveling around the world. They met non-Christian people with darker skin.

Colonists such as Christopher Columbus first came to the Americas in 1492. By 1600, they were at fault for more than 50 million Indigenous people's deaths.

Europeans wanted to mark themselves as different from these other peoples. They also wanted to justify the **colonization** of other peoples' lands. So, they began calling themselves *white*.

Race became another way to mark non-Christians as different and inferior. This became stronger across American colonies. European colonists kept calling themselves white. But they also created other races. Colonists called **Indigenous** people *savages* and other demeaning words. They enslaved African people and brought them to the Americas. Colonists called African people *subhuman*. These ideas led to the system of race. This system helped colonists justify the violent takeover of Indigenous lands. It also helped them justify the brutal enslavement of Black people.

⚠ Americans and Europeans captured, transported, and enslaved more than 12 million people from Africa.

The United States officially ended slavery after the Civil War (1861–1865). But conflict remained about the status of newly freed Black people, especially in the South. This period was known as Reconstruction. It lasted for more than 10 years. The US government aimed to give Black people equal rights, political power, and their own land. However, many white Americans resisted with racist violence.

Many Black people became sharecroppers. They often lived in debt to white landowners. A cycle of poverty began for many Black Americans. It has continued to affect them for generations.

In the 1870s, white lawmakers also started passing Jim Crow laws. These laws forced the separation of groups based on race. This is called segregation. Black people and white people used different schools, hospitals, and more. Many people challenged Jim Crow laws. But in 1896, the Supreme Court upheld segregation. The ruling helped strengthen **white supremacy** across the United States.

In the mid-1900s, Black Americans started the civil rights movement. Their mission was to fight for equality. They won victories throughout the 1950s and 1960s. These victories included ending Jim Crow laws.

▲ Ella Baker (left) was a key organizer of the civil rights movement.

Since then, the battle against racism has had highs and lows. In 2009, Barack Obama became the first Black president of the United States. Many people celebrated his win as a victory against racism. But in the early 2020s, the average wealth of white Americans was several times higher than that of Black and Latino Americans. Racism remained strong in the United States, even in the face of progress.

CASE STUDY

ANTI-ASIAN VIOLENCE

In early 2020, COVID-19 spread quickly around the world. No one knew exactly how COVID-19 had started. Scientists had guesses. But proving them would take months of research. In the meantime, some people made up their own stories about COVID-19. Many blamed China for the pandemic. That was because China had reported the first cases. Some people even suggested that China had created the virus on purpose.

These harmful rumors spread quickly. Some people who believed them began attacking Asian Americans. Hate crimes against Asian Americans soared. In the United States, there was a 77 percent increase from 2019 to 2020. Asian Americans were beaten and robbed. In a few cases, they were killed.

Racist violence harms individuals and the communities in which they live. In 2021, a news

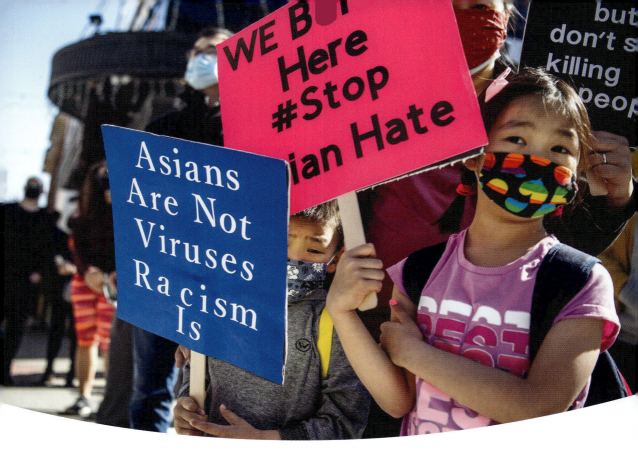

▲ Many people protested anti-Asian violence in 2021.

outlet polled Asian Americans. They were asked if they felt unsafe because of their race. More than half said they often felt unsafe.

Many lawmakers saw anti-Asian hate as a serious issue. In 2021, the US Congress passed the COVID-19 Hate Crimes Act. This law worked to improve hate crime reporting and prevention.

CHAPTER 3

CRIMINAL JUSTICE

Racism is often visible in the US criminal justice system. This is a system of rules, processes, and agencies. Together, they manage crime and enforce an area's laws.

On September 11, 2001, terrorists crashed airplanes into the World Trade Center and the Pentagon. Nearly 3,000 people died. The terrorists were members of al-Qaeda. This Islamic militant group is based in the Middle East.

The criminal justice system involves courts, prisons, police, and more.

After the attacks, many US law enforcement officials shifted focus. Some viewed certain citizens with more suspicion. Many Muslims became targeted. Many people of Middle Eastern and South Asian backgrounds did, too.

One program began in 2002. It asked men from 25 countries to register with the US government. Twenty-four of the 25 countries were Muslim-majority. More than 80,000 men were registered. Nearly 14,000 of them faced deportation. However, the program found zero terrorists.

This program used racial **profiling**. In racial profiling, people are suspected of crimes based on their race, religion, or nationality. Many studies show that people of color commit certain crimes at similar rates as white people. However, people of color are far more likely to be

▲ In the 2010s, people protested the New York Police Department's years-long spying on Muslim Americans.

arrested, while white people's crimes are more likely to be ignored.

Racism is also present during many arrests. Police brutality is one example. That's when police treat people with unnecessary violence. In 2020, a Minneapolis police officer murdered a Black man named George Floyd. This event led to protests around the world. The protests drew attention to a long-standing problem.

Police brutality affects white people, too. But non-white people are far more likely to be mistreated or even killed. Police brutality falls especially heavily on Indigenous people. Indigenous women are 38 times more likely to die in police encounters than white women.

Racism is also visible in US imprisonment rates. In 2022, 16 percent of the world's imprisoned people were in the United States. Yet the United States had only 4 percent of the world's population. Meanwhile, Black Americans were less than 14 percent of the US population. But they made up 38 percent of prisoners.

➤ THINK ABOUT IT

Do you think the police should ever consider a person's race or religion? Why or why not? Does your answer change depending on the crime?

▲ Some activists, like Angela Davis, argue that prisons and policing must be eliminated. They are called abolitionists.

Even after leaving prison, people still face many obstacles. Former prisoners can lose the right to vote. They can also lose parental rights and jobs. People who have been to prison are also 10 times more likely to be homeless.

CHAPTER 4

HOUSING AND WEALTH

In the early 1900s, many people started leaving the South. This included millions of Black Americans. They moved to cities such as New York, Los Angeles, and Chicago. They left the Jim Crow South. But they soon encountered racism outside the South, too. It was especially a problem with housing.

For years, banks openly wrote racism into **property deeds**. The deeds stated who was

Black Americans' journey to northern cities in the early 1900s was called the Great Migration.

allowed to own a property based on race. These bans were called racial covenants.

In the 1930s, the US government took these laws further. The government would not lend money to people of color to buy homes. It also refused to **insure** homes in non-white communities. The government marked these neighborhoods red on its maps. This practice became known as redlining. Without insurance, non-white neighborhoods suffered from neglect.

The United States banned redlining and racial covenants in 1968. But forms of housing discrimination continued. For example, reverse redlining began in the 1990s. In reverse redlining, lenders target low-income and non-white neighborhoods. They give people unfair loans. These loans often have high interest rates. That makes the loans hard to pay off.

▲ Foreclosure makes it harder for people to borrow money in the future. It can also make it harder to get a job.

Reverse redlining can be devastating. For example, Black homeowners face a higher risk of **foreclosure**. This is true even when they live in white neighborhoods. Owning a home is often a key step in building wealth. But as of the early 2020s, Black and Latino Americans owned homes at far lower rates than white Americans.

CHAPTER 5

HEALTH AND MEDICINE

The United States has one of the world's most advanced health-care systems. But not everyone experiences it in the same way. Institutional racism creates health **inequities**. They appear in health outcomes, life expectancy, and more.

Racism can start to affect people's health at birth. In the United States, Black infants are more than twice as likely to die as white infants.

In 2021, nearly 20 percent of Latino Americans did not have health insurance, compared to 7 percent of white Americans.

Some racism in health care is based on outdated science. For example, scientists once believed people of different races were biologically different. This idea produced **stereotypes** that still exist today.

One of these stereotypes involves pain. Some people believe Black people don't feel pain as

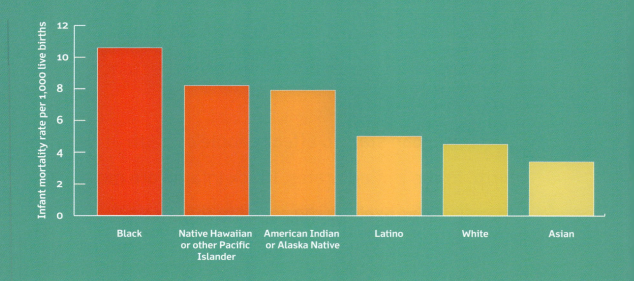

INFANT MORTALITY RATES BY RACE AND ETHNICITY

much as white people. This belief is false. But the idea still causes real harm. Doctors are less likely to give pain medication to Black patients than they are to white patients. This is true even when patients have the same illness. When Black patients do receive pain medication, they receive smaller amounts. Even young children can experience inequality in pain treatment.

Other health threats are outside the hospital. Many dangers are in the environment. Hazards can include polluted air or unsafe drinking water. They can also include a lack of healthy food options. These conditions are more common near communities of color. They often lead to poor health. This is known as environmental racism.

Environmental racism has many causes. Suppose a Black family buys a home in a redlined area of their city. City officials decide to build a landfill in that area. This landfill causes the neighborhood's property values to drop. The Black family wants to move. But no one will pay a fair price for their house. The family faces a terrible choice. They can live near a toxic landfill. Or they can lose money on the sale of their home.

Environmental racism can cause public health crises. In 2022, Jackson, Mississippi, experienced several days of heavy rain. Rainwater flooded the city's sewers. That caused the main water treatment plant to fail. For months, residents had to boil their tap water. That was the only way to make the water safe for drinking.

This was not the first time Jackson's water system had failed. Many people, including the city's mayor, blamed institutional racism. Jackson is a majority-Black city. In contrast, many of Mississippi's political leaders are white.

▲ A woman in Jackson, Mississippi, uses boiled water to safely clean her dishes.

Critics argued that the state's leaders had purposely kept money from the city. They said Jackson had needed that money for decades. In October 2022, the US Congress opened an investigation. Congress wanted to know if Mississippi had wrongly held back federal money from Jackson.

CHAPTER 6

EDUCATION

Racism exists in schools, too. For example, it affects how students are punished. Children of color are not more likely to misbehave than white students. But they are more likely to be suspended or expelled. When students are kept out of school, they can't learn. They can fall behind on schoolwork. It can start a cycle of failing grades. A suspension or expulsion in childhood can make it harder to finish school later on.

Disruptive behaviors in school often happen because a student's needs are not being met.

Many schools use "zero-tolerance" policies with students of color. These rules often treat minor problems like crimes. Some schools even involve police in disciplining students. This can do lasting harm to the students who experience it.

Another way racism affects students is through the opportunity gap. The opportunity gap describes the importance of race or place

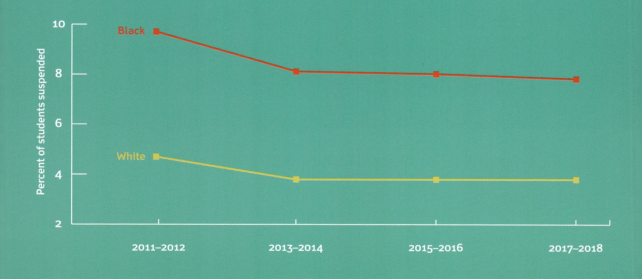

SCHOOL SUSPENSIONS BY RACE

of birth in education. These uncontrollable factors can create **disparity** in academic support and performance. It most often describes gaps between white students and students of color.

For example, studies have looked at schools with a high number of low-income students and students of color. These schools often have lower-quality textbooks, larger class sizes, and less-qualified teachers. As a result, these students tend to score lower on math and reading tests. Children with low math and reading skills are more likely to be held back a grade or not graduate at all.

THINK ABOUT IT ◁

What are some discipline methods that would encourage students to stay in school?

CASE STUDY

THE CROWN ACT

In March 2021, four-year-old Jett Hawkins was going to a school in Chicago, Illinois. That month, he asked his mother to braid his hair. He wanted a new hairstyle for school. When she finished, Jett loved the way he looked. But an administrator said the braids broke a school policy. Students at Jett's school weren't allowed to wear natural Black hairstyles such as locs, twists, or braids.

Jett's mother shared his story with news reporters. When a state senator heard about Jett, he proposed a new law to end hair discrimination in schools. The Jett Hawkins Law went into effect in January 2022. This meant Illinois schools could no longer have dress codes based on hairstyles.

This law was similar to laws that other states had recently passed. California was the first state to pass such a law. It passed in 2019. By 2022, many states had passed laws to end hair

▲ In one study, one-third of Black students in majority-white schools faced hair discrimination.

discrimination. Most of these laws were called the CROWN Act.

CROWN stands for Creating a Respectful and Open World for Natural Hair. The CROWN Act makes it illegal to deny work or educational opportunities to someone because of their hair texture or style.

CHAPTER 7

FIGHTING RACISM

Racism might seem like an impossible problem to solve. And it's true that people will never get rid of all racism everywhere. But there are many people working hard to fight racism every day. Activists attack this big problem from many directions. Research, protests, and lawmaking are just a few ways people are tackling the issue.

In 2016, a team of scholars and activists started the Mapping Prejudice project.

Working together with large groups of people can be an effective way to fight racism.

Mapping Prejudice researches old property records. Members work to uncover evidence of racial covenants. Then they add that information to an online map. The group started by creating a map of racial covenants in Hennepin County, Minnesota. The map was the first of its kind in the United States. It helps residents understand systemic racism. That way, people can better understand how racism continues to impact their neighborhoods today.

A wave of protests pushed a professional sports team to change its racist name. The name of the Washington, DC, football team once had an anti-Native slur. For decades, Indigenous activists had demanded the team change its name. The team ignored the calls for change until 2020. That summer, George Floyd's murder at the hands of police officers started a wave of protests.

▲ Clyde Bellecourt was an Indigenous activist who led calls to change the Washington football team's name.

Activists called for an end to racism, especially within institutions. Sports teams, including Washington's, couldn't ignore the issue anymore. For two years, they played as the Washington Football Team. In 2022, they changed their name to the Washington Commanders.

▲ Young people are often important voices in struggles against racism.

US lawmakers continue to introduce bills to ensure fairness for people of all races. In June 2022, Senator Alex Padilla introduced a new bill. It was called the Fairness for Farm Workers Act (FFA). The bill was written to update an older law, the 1938 Fair Labor Standards Act. The Fair Labor Standards Act guaranteed workers certain rights and protections. But farmworkers were kept out of the bill. That was because most farmworkers weren't white. If passed, the FFA would ensure farmworkers receive fair pay for their work, regardless of race.

There are many ways for young people to take action. People can call out racism when they see or hear it. They can share stories about the people fighting racism. They can also read more about how racism affects communities. Then they can share what they learn with others.

THINK ABOUT IT ◁

What are some ways you could fight racism in your community?

FOCUS ON
RACISM

Write your answers on a separate piece of paper.

1. Write a paragraph describing one example of racism in the health-care industry and how it impacts people.

2. Do you find it easy or hard to talk about racism? Why do you think that is?

3. In what year did the football team in Washington, DC, change its name to the Washington Commanders?

    A. 2016
    B. 2020
    C. 2022

4. Why would systemic racism be the hardest type to eliminate?

    A. It uses a scientific system.
    B. It involves all parts of society.
    C. It started very recently.

Answer key on page 48.

GLOSSARY

colonization
When one country controls another group of people in a different area and uses those people and their land for the country's benefit.

disparity
A difference or lack of equality.

foreclosure
A process in which a lender takes a property from a homeowner who can no longer make payments.

Indigenous
Native to a region, or belonging to ancestors who lived in a region before colonists arrived.

inequities
Unfair differences or imbalances.

insure
To cover certain costs, such as medical treatment or home damage.

profiling
Targeting a person based on their physical traits or actions.

property deeds
Legal documents that change who owns houses or other properties.

stereotypes
Oversimplified, unfair, or untrue ideas about what all members of a certain group are like.

white supremacy
The system that gives unfair power and privileges to white people, upheld by the belief that white people are better than people of other races.

TO LEARN MORE

BOOKS

Diggs, Barbara. *Race Relations: The Struggle for Equality in America.* White River Junction, VT: Nomad Press, 2019.

Dyson, Michael Eric, and Marc Favreau. *Unequal: A Story of America.* New York: Little, Brown and Company, 2022.

Jewell, Tiffany. *This Book Is Anti-Racist: 20 Lessons on How to Wake Up, Take Action, and Do the Work*. Minneapolis: Frances Lincoln Children's Books, 2020.

NOTE TO EDUCATORS

Visit **www.focusreaders.com** to find lesson plans, activities, links, and other resources related to this title.

INDEX

Civil War, 13
COVID-19, 16–17
CROWN Act, 39

environmental racism, 31–32

Floyd, George, 21, 42

institutional racism, 8–9, 29, 32, 43
interpersonal racism, 8

Jackson, Mississippi, 32–33
Jett Hawkins Law, 38
Jim Crow, 14, 25

Mapping Prejudice, 41–42

Padilla, Alex, 44
Puerto Rico, 8

racial profiling, 20
Reconstruction, 13

schools, 9, 14, 35–37, 38
systemic racism, 9, 42

Washington Commanders, 43
Williams, Serena, 5–6

Answer Key: 1. Answers will vary; **2.** Answers will vary; **3.** C; **4.** B